DISCOVERING SEA LIONS

Lorijo Metz

PowerKiDS press
New York

To Dwight, for your lionlike roar and your puppy-dog face

Published in 2012 by The Rosen Publishing Group, Inc.
29 East 21st Street, New York, NY 10010

First Edition

Editor: Amelie von Zumbusch
Book Design: Kate Laczynski

Photo Credits: Cover Steve Allen/Getty Images; pp. 4–5 © www.iStockphoto.com/Carol Gering; p. 6 Sue Flood/Getty Images; pp. 7 (top), 10, 14, 16–17, 19 Shutterstock.com; pp. 7 (bottom), 11 (bottom) John Foxx/Stockbyte/Thinkstock; p. 8 Reinhard Dirscherl/Getty Images; p. 9 Joel Sartore/Getty Images; pp. 11 (top), 12 iStockphoto/Thinkstock; p. 13 Panoramic Images/Getty Images; p. 15 (top, bottom) Arthur Morris/Getty Images; p. 18 Yoshikazu Tsuno/AFP/Getty Images; p. 20 Sandy Huffaker/Getty Images; p. 21 Don MacKinnon/Getty Images; p. 22 Jason Edwards/Getty Images.

Library of Congress Cataloging-in-Publication Data

Metz, Lorijo.
  Discovering sea lions / by Lorijo Metz. — 1st ed.
    p. cm. — (Along the shore)
  ISBN 978-1-4488-4992-5 (library binding)
  1. Sea lions—Juvenile literature. I. Title.
  QL737.P63M48 2012
  599.79'75—dc22
                              2010047570

Manufactured in the United States of America

CPSIA Compliance Information: Batch #WS11PK: For Further Information contact Rosen Publishing, New York, New York at 1-800-237-9932

CONTENTS

WHAT ARE SEA LIONS?

Some people think sea lions get their name from the lionlike mane many of the males have. Others say it is their lionlike roar. It is not likely that you would really mistake a sea lion for a lion. Sea lions are often mistaken for seals, though. That is because sea lions, seals, and walruses all belong to a group of animals called **pinnipeds**. The word "pinniped" means "**flipper** footed." All pinnipeds have four flippers. Their strong, paddlelike flippers help them swim.

Although pinnipeds live in the water, they are not fish. Like cows, horses, and people, pinnipeds are **mammals**. As all mammals do, pinnipeds breathe air.

Sea lions live in the ocean most of the time. However, they also spend time on sandy beaches and rocky shorelines.

WHERE DO SEA LIONS LIVE?

Sea lions live both on land and in the ocean. You can find them in every ocean except the Atlantic. On land, they like rocky shores or sandy beaches backed by cliffs.

There are several **species**, or kinds, of sea lions. South American sea lions, Australian sea lions, and New Zealand sea lions live in the Southern **Hemisphere**, or the southern half of Earth.

Steller sea lions are the largest kind of sea lions. Some male Steller sea lions weigh more than 1 ton (1 t).

Sea lions also live in the Northern Hemisphere. California sea lions make their homes along North America's Pacific coast, from Mexico to British Columbia. Steller sea lions like colder waters. While some live on the California coast, most favor the icy waters around Alaska and the Bering Sea.

Galápagos sea lions live around the Galápagos Islands. These islands are along the equator, where the Northern Hemisphere and Southern Hemisphere meet.

WHAT DO SEA LIONS LOOK LIKE?

Sea lions are covered in short, thin hairs. Their tube-shaped bodies are perfect for swimming and diving. Their coats come in many shades of brown. When their fur is wet, it looks shiny and almost black.

Sea lions' large **foreflippers**, or front flippers, look like wings. Sea lions move quickly through the water by moving their

Sea lions' powerful flippers and smooth shape make them great swimmers. Sea lions are fast and can move easily in the water.

Sea lions often leap into the water, as these animals are doing. Sea lions sometimes leap out of the water, too.

foreflippers up and down in smooth, winglike movements. Their **hind flippers**, or back flippers, are flat with five long, webbed toes. Sea lions use their hind flippers to direct their movements in the water. On land, sea lions fold their hind flippers beneath their bodies to help them walk.

SEA LION FACT

Sea lions have long, pointed snouts, or noses, with whiskers. Many people think that this makes them look like dogs.

9

SEA LION OR SEAL?

How do you know if you are looking at a sea lion or a seal? Look at the animal's ears. Sea lions have small ear flaps on the sides of their heads. Seals have only tiny openings.

The two animals also move differently on land. Sea lions turn their hind flippers forward and scoot over rocky shores and sand. Seals cannot turn their hind flippers. They hold them out

You can tell that this pinniped is a sea lion by the ways its ears stick out and by the way it is resting on its flippers.

California harbor seals live in many of the same places as California sea lions. This seal's short foreflippers make it easy to recognize, though.

straight behind them, roll from side to side, and slide over land on their bellies.

Sea lions' and seals' foreflippers are different, too. Sea lions have wide, hairless foreflippers that look like wings. Seals have short, fur-covered foreflippers with long claws.

Note the ear openings on this seal. If you look at the sea lion on page 10, it is easy to see the differences in these pinnipeds' ears.

HUNTING AND FOOD

Sea lions hunt mostly at night. They hunt either alone or with a few other sea lions. They feast on all kinds of ocean animals, from crabs to small sharks. In the Southern Hemisphere, sea lions also eat penguins.

Sea lions may dive as deep as 600 feet (183 m) in search of food. Down that deep in the ocean,

This sea lion has caught and is eating a salmon. Fish, such as salmon, are one of the most important foods for sea lions.

Sea lions can stay underwater for several minutes before coming up to breathe. This gives them plenty of time to find a meal.

it is cold and dark. Beneath their skin, sea lions have a thick layer of **blubber**, or fat. This keeps them warm. Sea lions see well underwater. They use their whiskers to sense fish in the dark, deep part of the ocean, though.

SEA LION FACT

Sea lions do not need to drink water. The fish they eat supply all the water they need.

SEA LION PUPS

Female adult sea lions are called cows. Cows have one **pup**, or baby, every year. Pups arrive with their eyes open, ready to drink their mothers' milk.

While cows hunt, pups stay together in **rookeries**. There, one of the mothers watches over the pups as they sleep and play. Though rookeries are loud, pups always recognize their mothers' voices.

Sea lion pups have black or dark brown fur. Newborn pups are about 30 inches (76 cm) long. The pups grow quickly.

Pups drink their mothers' milk for between six months and a year. The milk has a lot of fat in it. This helps the pups grow quickly.

Shortly after they are born, pups have their first swimming and fishing lessons. Pups stay with their mothers for up to three years. The pups have much to learn, such as how to stay away from sharks.

Sea lion pups are born on land. The pups begin to walk about half an hour after they are born.

LIVING WITH SEA LIONS

SEA LION FACT

A large group of sea lions on land is called a colony. A group of sea lions in the water is called a raft.

Sea lions often return to the same place every year to give birth. While they are there, **harems**, or families, form. A harem has around 15 cows and their pups. It has just one bull, or male sea lion. Often, several harems live in one spot.

If you were walking along the shore and there were sea lions ahead, you would likely hear them before you saw them. Sea lions are

Several harems of South American sea lions are sharing this rocky beach. The males are the large ones with the puffy manes.

always barking, roaring, and climbing over each other. The bulls bark very loudly when they are guarding their harems.

After about three months, bulls return to the ocean in search of better fishing places. The cows and pups stay behind, though.

CALIFORNIA SEA LIONS

Have you ever seen a trained "seal" jumping through hoops or balancing a ball on its nose? More often than not, animals that are called trained seals are really California sea lions. California sea lions are friendly, playful, and smart. They are easy to train. In fact, they are

This California sea lion is doing a trick. It is part of a show at the Hakkeijima Sea Paradise, in Tokyo, Japan.

Sea lions are good at doing things with their front flippers. They can use these flippers to pick things up, shake hands, and wave.

the species of sea lion most often used in **circuses** and other animal shows.

In the wild, friendly California sea lions like to gather in large groups. They are the fastest swimmers of all sea lions. They can speed through water at up to 25 miles per hour (40 km/h)!

BEYOND HOOPS AND BALLS

The U.S. Navy has been training sea lions and other pinnipeds since 1960. They have trained sea lions to recognize and bring back objects that were dropped in the ocean. In many cases, recovering these objects would be unsafe for people. However, sea lions are better divers than people are. They can do the job quickly and safely.

These sailors in the Navy are welcoming a hard-working sea lion back to their boat. They are on a training exercise near San Diego, California.

Here you can see a sea lion wearing a harness. The harness is made so that it does not get in the way while the sea lion is swimming.

13K 95396

SEA LION FACT

Depending on their species, sea lions can hold their breath underwater for between 8 and 20 minutes.

By wearing a special **harness**, or belt, sea lions can carry underwater cameras. The pictures they send back help keep our oceans safe in times of war. Trainers also plan to use sea lions with cameras to find divers who get trapped underwater.

HOW ARE SEA LIONS DOING?

People once hunted sea lions for their skin, oil, and whiskers. This is now against the law in many places. However, that does not always stop people from hunting them. In some places, people have caught so many fish that there are few left for sea lions to eat. Sea lions can also get caught in fishing nets.

Sadly, Galápagos sea lions, such as this one, are endangered. This means they are in danger of dying out.

In recent years, people have worked to make the world safe for sea lions. Some species, such as the California sea lion, have now grown in number.

blubber (BLUH-ber) The fat of a whale, penguin, or other sea animal.

circuses (SUR-kus-ez) Shows at which people and animals do tricks.

flipper (FLIH-per) A wide, flat body part that helps certain animals swim.

foreflippers (FAWR-flih-perz) Front flippers.

harems (HER-emz) Groups with one male and many females.

harness (HAR-nes) The ties, bands, and other pieces that hold something or someone in place.

hemisphere (HEH-muh-sfeer) Half of a round object.

hind flippers (HYND FLIH-perz) Back flippers.

mammals (MA-mulz) Warm-blooded animals that have backbones and hair, breathe air, and feed milk to their young.

pinnipeds (PIH-nuh-pedz) A group of animals that have flippers instead of legs.

pup (PUP) A type of baby animal.

rookeries (RUK-er-eez) Places where young animals grow up together.

species (SPEE-sheez) One kind of living thing. All people are one species.

INDEX

WEB SITES

Due to the changing nature of Internet links, PowerKids Press has developed an online list of Web sites related to the subject of this book. This site is updated regularly. Please use this link to access the list:

www.powerkidslinks.com/alsh/sealion/